W9-ABC-572

Fragments From Our Heritage

MICHAEL GRAZNAK

Reiman Publications, Inc. Milwaukee, Wisconsin

Library of Congress Number 75-17123

Copyright © 1975   Reiman Publications, Inc.

In Dedication

Once more I bring

wilted flowers

to my mother

Listen

Some say the wind plays tricks
on old ears.
At times one fancies that he hears
the ancient tone
of the mountain dulcimer speaking
its rural poetry.
It echoes up the valleys
to the mountain peaks
and beyond
then is gone.
Today the wind sings;
I hear the sound of those strings.
Listen!
Listen, listen . . .

Dear brothers and sisters

The long thin fingers of the ash tree

where the turkeys roosted

write a message on the sky:

Come home—

Rest now.

Listen to the katydids when the sun is down

behind the chestnut tree on Garrison's Hill.

Listen to father's whistle

as he hoes

the last row of corn before dark.

Hear mother's, "That's enough work for today, John."

Bill the mule and Babe the mare

are clopping down the hill

as Bessie's bell rings from Barbrick's Hollow;

the herd follows . . .

then it is still again.

The oil lamp flickers in the kitchen.

Grass in the yard grows damp.

The dewy moisture frees

potato-bread scents from the brick oven

where mother baked.

Already the lightning bugs spark

the dark edges of the woods.

The message of the ash fades fast—

We grow old.

Come home.

Time

In a little wooden church

now long gone

we spoke to God

in word and song.

A tired farmer

in the pastor's role

sang "Beautiful Zion."

A small boy

with his eye on

the clock

blinked

and it was today.

Soil

*"Soil is rock on its way
to the sea"—W.A. Albrecht*

Restless soil,

mother and grave

of all that lived

and all life

yet to be,

why must you forever

move to the sea?

Restless clay,

as man or rock

blade of grass or albatross,

before you move on,

know that I see

that I am you

and you are me.

Banjo Lee

Banjo Lee was our neighbor.

He played and sang

for the thresher gang

in loud and rustic flavor.

I almost cried when he sang

"The Little Rosewood Casket",

and "Bury Me Not On The Lone Prairie".

Then came "Oh Susanna",

and "Darling Nelly Gray",

as I slipped away into slumber.

Today when a symphony plays,

and that silence falls

before the applause,

I still hear strong,

one clear note from a banjo.

Buzzard

The buzzard,
seen up close
is not
a thing of beauty.
His low calling
gets no praise
as he goes
about his duty
recycling garbage
and spent bodies.
Few know
that we owe
him an apology.
For his may be
the first ecology.

Natural Foods

Coarse

rough breads,

stone ground meal

or whole wheat biscuits

are the rage now.

Yet,

I clearly recall

when store-bought bread,

for sandwiches at lunch

was the envy of the bunch

whose home-baked fare

with Damson plum jam

was eaten in shame

behind the schoolhouse.

Witchcraft

I knew there was a witch

locked up in the trunk of a tree

in our yard.

I thought that maybe I'd be rich

if I could set her free.

I brewed a small boy's spell

from mud and flour and cow manure

I mixed my potion well.

At night beneath October's moon

I made up chants and sounds

that stirred the chickens on their roosts—

still my witch was tightly bound.

Instead, I lured my sister . . .

She took a tragic step

into my magic

and turned my exorcism

into end-warming rhythms

played by my father's hand.

Old Folks

The schoolhouse is gone,

our church stands no more,

the sayings that guided

our ways are now quaint.

Those who know

are afraid to bore,

so our faces wrinkle

from restraint.

The Klutz

A three-dollar Sears guitar

complete with pages of diagrams

showing how the notes should be fretted

failed to make me a musician.

Then I tried

starting my own mine

but after a long time of digging

a cow tore down my rigging.

I'll never hear the end

of when

the umbrella broke

terminating my acrobatic endeavors—

my failures went on forever.

Today as I walk, adult at last,

looking back to a past

so fraught with bad examples,

I trample

my neighbor's flowers.

Monarch

He,

who leads this fragile form,

this delicate mother of a worm,

for a thousand miles and more

fed,

rested

and unharmed,

must surely have a plan

of equal worth

for man.

My Little Girl

We were not strangers

before we met—

I knew a name to say.

I saw your smile

a thousand times

in flowers that found a way

to cheer me.

From old fashioned blooms

in school books of former days

to desert flowers

and well-tended ways

of hollyhocks

that drew praise in formal gardens

I hear a little girl's voice

laugh near me.

A Secret

A tiny twig

pinched from a coveted plant

hides securely

in the palm of her hand

and hurries home.

It finds a way to grow roots

and shoots

into a full grown rose . . .

and nobody knows

that my mother steals flowers.

Look

Those who laugh

at robins

seeking worms in the snow,

need only know

that sometimes

they find them.

Milling Day

Going to the mill took all day

but it had to be done to get flour.

Dad would decide

whose turn it was to ride,

while

mother made a lunch to eat

when the wagon ferried the river.

On the way home

came an icecream cone,

vanilla flavored;

every lick savored,

to last

as it has

in my mind . . .

for a lifetime.

Old Sayings

The wheel that squeaks the loudest

is the one that gets the grease.

What is sauce for the gander

is also sauce for the geese.

Early to bed and early to rise

or pulling the wool

over someone's eyes.

These old expressions

and other rural professions

are almost gone now.

Soon our children will be asking,

"Old saw, now what does that mean?"

Dog of the Road

Sad, skinny tail-drooping

dog on the road,

as you sniff at trash

or eat a car-mangled rabbit

in the safety of a ditch,

did you know a warm home

where pups grew up?

"A farm family will find you,"

they said.

Then you heard the heartless sound

of tires that ground the road

while you stood in the dark and cold,

a new dog of the road.

Old Stone Home

Bruised knuckles,

blistered hands;

days of rain and chilling cold.

Lifting,

fitting and trying again,

man alone,

wresting security from stone.

He won.

For a moment,

a work of art,

a pride

in work well done.

He rested,

cared for a family,

grew old and moved on.

Now stones slide slowly

one from the other

into the sod

from which he borrowed them—

back to God.

Light

Shine,
happy light
of lamp and youth
into every corner;
wash clean
the darkness
and show us the truth.

Smile with Me

Because I now laugh

at the time a calf

upset a bucket in a barn

now marked only by a spot

of dark green grass,

you call me old.

When I speak of a team

you smile when I mean

things like wagons and harness

or reins that I used to hold,

you call me old.

You laugh

When I take off my hat

as the flag goes by

or a lady's eye

notes the barren head

that once had hair.

Still I smile,

for one tomorrow soon,

you will laugh

at your own team and calf.

To the Last of the Whooping Cranes

Crane,

what secret do you carry

as you glide in the twilight

of your time?

What message do your numbered

wingbeats whisper

of a long ago

that we cannot know?

Wind

When I envied

the freedom of the breeze

to dance in the grass

or sing in the trees,

I recalled the cruelty that he sees

from age to age—

the Valley Forges,

the cold jagged rocks

of mountain gorges.

While he moves the sand

to hide unmarked graves

in a nameless land,

I ask

who can deny him

an occasional pine to sigh in

or the chance

to play games with a seagull?

My Prairie

Prairie,

you felt the aching hooves

of oxen

pulling a family's hopes

toward a distant promise.

Onto your soil

fell freightened tears.

A dented rifle ball sinks deeper

beside a broken arrowhead.

A tooth remains

of one who broke a slave's chains

but fell

the prey of his freedom.

Each season

your pen writes anew,

but scratches out a few

of yesterday's words.

Nature

When I was a small boy
an old tree died in our yard.
I tried hard to understand
as mother took my hand
and explained,
"It will turn to ground.
Then God will make a tree
from that soil."
In a single breath
I knew life and death
and my first miracle.

I Hear

Tell me how a mouse

with small sharp teeth

picks out the heart

of a grain of wheat

or a worm,

too small to see,

knows

what to eat

and what to let be.

Tell me how a chick hatches

or seeds grow in a pod

and I will hear you

speak of God.

Boardinghouse Bench

The boardinghouse bench
from Rosedale mine
was given to my father
at the time
of the great depression.
It had served a succession
of lonely immigrant men
who ate their meals
as they told their tales
of the old country.
Fourteen of us
children grew up
seated on bench
at the kitchen table,
six at a time.
Each grew so unlike the other
that I once heard mother ask,
"Could it be that those men
left their intents
impressed on that old bench?"

Symphony from a Flight Of Wild Geese

A faint chord whispers

in the distance

then grows by measure

until the skies sing.

High notes ring a crescendo;

then depart

as the calendar of God bids,

until one faint chord

dies in the distance

leaving only spring.

Initials

The initials he carved

when he climbed the beech

are much too high

for an old man to reach.

He put them there

deep and clear

to mark his age.

Now as he reads

that small boy's pride

carved in the bark

he prays;

May there be beeches

and a Barlow knife

in every boy's life.

May he climb high while he can.

There is time enough

on the ground

as a man.

A Lady

A smile

to ease the tension

when daily cares are pressing—

a light touch

shows she cares.

A quiet voice,

as the world grows louder . . .

she understands

as she works miracles

with her hands.

When the Young And Old Talk

Truth springs

from an exchange—

of the wisdom

of youth

for the knowledge

of age.

We Knew What We Liked

We studied abstract design

somehow

on the flank of a Holstein cow.

Delicate unsigned masters

were not lacking

on river banks

where drying mud was cracking

or fallen flower petals

were winning medals

for their textural polychromes.

Mobiles

hanging from spider webs

put on multi-media shows

with authentic natural sounds.

Man-made?

Not even one part.

<u>That</u> was art.

Mother's Lessons

I learned love

when mama shook the tree

to make it rain

cold and tickley on my face.

She held me tight

when I threw stones

to splash big circles in the creek.

Mother spoke of being kind

of trying to find

the good.

I understood

for we talked a lot

but not

nearly enough

to last all of my years.

Fog

Fog,

as I walk to see

what splendor you hide,

you move your web

to cloak another

more promising wonder,

until I step into your fold.

Your soft veil

masking that which lies beyond,

keeps me asking,

do you show me life

or invite me to a fool's game.

The Sportsman

Why must a man enslave

the beauty that gave

him pleasure?

Why must he destroy

as he commands

the blazing power to shoot?

Then

when he sees the dead mass

of bleeding feathers

turns to search the skies

for more?

Promise

Through the bitter winter's blast
you stood forgotten,
your dark garment
tight about your form
like some old monk,
silent,
devout
and cold.
Then a warm breath whispered
from the south
and gentle fingers
began unwinding
your drab bindings
to show what treasure
you were hiding.

Death of an Elm

Rattle your bare bones,

old tree,

rattle your own elegy

until the final thud

when you drop to earth . . .

to become earth,

as does the virus

that takes you to your silence.

Sound an elegy

then go

to those who knew the joys of your time . . .

hide your name where theirs is hidden;

rest well my elm.

Wheat

Limp spaghetti,

drowning in grease

in the sloppy land of buffet.

If the wheat crop had failed

you would not be flailed

on a plate

by some self-styled gourmet.

Father's Advice

Son,

do not anguish for words

to say, "I love you dad".

They can never be your own.

Just be yourself

and what you mean

will be clearly shown.

Kitten

Priceless treasure

soft and warm

given

secretly

behind the barn,

without a parent's permission.

Who's

to break the sad news

that a pet

is too much trouble?

Displaced Farmer

All I know
is an iron hoe
and a weed
from a cotton plant.
Now you say
I must go away—
there's no room
for me on the land.
Go?
Go where?

All I know
is how to pray
for a rain
to save the crop.
Now you say
I must go away
and yet
my prayers don't stop.
Go?
Go where?

Father's Plow

My father's old plow
speaks clearly of how
the two of them
followed straining horses
day by day
putting furrow on furrow
along the hillside.
Still he knew pride,
or whatever it was
that guided his cause
and his furrows to plowed fields,
to crops and harvests,
and back to one slow furrow after another
until a buried rock
tore the handles from his hands.

Accidental Sculpture

Men tear the rock

from its roots

with dynamite that thunders

to reveal

a face of stone

or other hidden wonders.

Learning

I watched uncle Joe

sharpen the scythe

with swinging strokes of the stone

until it would cut

when it touched

a blade of grass.

When I tried

to hone the scythe

it dulled more with every stroke

until he taught me

that stone and steel

should be friends.

Work

Days were lean

when a pot of beans

warmed from yesterday's lunch

was the only food on the table.

Still they spoke not of despair,

only that their

new crop had not come in yet.

With one set of clothes

they did not feel poor

even if their neighbors had more.

The hard luck of some

was overcome

by work

in the ways explained in their bible.

They died

rich with the pride

of providing for their own survival.

Just Be

If children could be free

to run and laugh,

free of the webs that bind them,

free of clouds to shade their mirth

and free to keep the wisdom that comes with birth.

If they could learn from trees and earth

then their children might be free

to be—

just be.

Country Noises

The bluebells ring so loud.

Purple phloxes crowd and shout

toward puffy clouds.

Baby foxes yelp under trees

that stage-whisper for silence.

One bird applauds the song of another.

The dogwood's bark

is lost in the rhythm

of the Jack-in-the-pulpit's prayer

near the ditch

where water babbles

to noisy ducks in the gravel;

City, it's not surprising—

I just can't hear your siren call

at all.

The Unknown

He dreaded the things
that thought would be
if the man who raised goats
across the sea
came to be his neighbor.
He was not prejudiced—
only afraid.

Coal Patch Blacksmith

The smoke that soared

from his ancient forge

could be seen for miles away.

Everyone heard

when his hammer rang,

its silence marked

the end of day.

He knew every horse, every house

every child that could toddle.

But his friends were few

so no one knew

just where he hid his bottle.

Look Again

The humble one
who dares to look
beneath the stones
on the bed of a brook
as he did
through the eyes of a child,
will see God's plan
through the eyes of a man.

Sweet Sounds

Today,

or when I finally go home,

to toil

or walk in memory;

let there be the music

of God's creatures

telling me in their simple way

that I am never alone.

My Wish

One cold distant night

when ice crackles in the tree

over a small mound of snow

that is me;

When the paper

that bore these words

no longer is—

may a poet walk

warm with the thought

of some words that are his—

all his.